#POST THIS BOOK

DAVID SINDEN & NIKALAS CATLOW

sourcebooks
fire

Published by Sourcebooks Fire, an imprint of Sourcebooks, Inc.
P.O. Box 4410, Naperville, Illinois 60567-4410
(630) 961-3900
Fax: (630) 961-2168
www.sourcebooks.com

Originally published as Post This in 2015 in the United Kingdom by Macmillan
Children's Books, an imprint of Pan Macmillan.

Library of Congress Cataloging-in-Publication data is on file with the publisher.

Printed and bound in the United States of America.
VP 10 9 8 7 6 5 4 3 2 1

Also by David Sinden &and Nikalas Catlow

Anti Journal

You can share photos and videos online instantly and they can be a really great way to connect with friends and let the world know what you're doing. But it's worth remembering it can be difficult and often impossible to delete pictures or videos from the Internet entirely. Once you share something online, you lose control of it—it can be copied and shared further. And you're sharing it with more than just your friends. Anyone and everyone can see it. Think twice before posting something you might later regret.

This book will spark your creativity
and fill your social media feed
with creative, fun images.

Respond to its prompts in any way
you wish, whether on or off its pages:
by filming, photographing,
drawing, or making.

Express yourself without need for
perfection and post all images with
the hashtag #PostThisBook

Explore the hashtag to see how others
use this book to spark their creativity.

Capture yourself holding this book for the first time, before life changes.

📷 Take a photo

and **POST** it with the hashtag **#POST THIS BOOK**

I AM HERE

#PostThisBook

Point this arrow. Take a selfie of where you are now. **POST IT.**

Complete and share this: **#POST THIS BOOK**

"**Me in 3 words**"

___Nice_____

___Funny_____

___Caring_____

Fill this square in
any way you like

 #POST THIS BOOK Square compare

Attempt to draw a
PIG IN A WIG

#POST THIS BOOK

Post a photograph
that plays with light

#POST THIS BOOK

Create
outside
this book.

Paint an egg.

Share it #POST THIS BOOK

Take a 360-
degree video

#PostThisBook

Grow this seed #POST THIS BOOK

WHAM BAM KERPOW!

Express yourself as if you lived in a comic

Tag a friend

BFF

#POST THIS BOOK

TRANSFORM YOUR SELFIE

#POST THIS BOOK

Point and snap

Respond to each of the prompts below. Create on the pages of this book or outside it using any medium you like.

LINES

ADD EYES TO ANY OBJECT

A view through a cardboard tube

#POST THIS BOOK

AN IMAGE INSPIRED BY GOOGLING THE WORD STRIPES

SHOUTY EDDIE

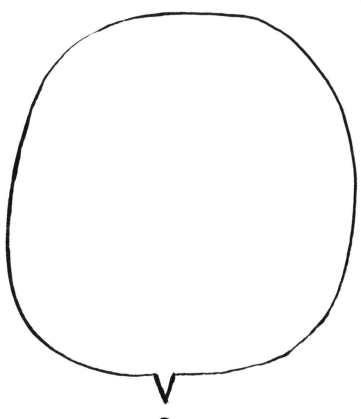

Make him shout

IN MY DREAMS

📷 POINT

CHILLING

HEALTHY!

& SNAP #POST THIS BOOK

TICKETS

FILM THIS

FILLING UP

#POST THIS BOOK

#POST THIS BOOK MUG SHOT

Customize then hold your personal mug

↑

While creating with this book, treat
every in-between or leftover space
as a canvas, however small.
Doodle, pattern, and color around
things. Fill up the background.
#EverySpaceUsed

→

Film fast food

#POST THIS BOOK

or food going fast

#POST THIS BOOK Decorate stones

#POST THIS BOOK Show a worthless thing you love

GRAVITY IN ACTION

Decorate
a branch

Hat on
a pet

#POST
THIS
BOOK

WHAT DOES A SNIGLET LOOK LIKE?

#POST THIS BOOK

Stack your books #POST THIS BOOK

Rehome this penguin in the outside world. Photograph it in its new habitat. #POST THIS BOOK

UpdateYourPage

Make a new profile pic #POST THIS BOOK

#POST THIS BOOK

Turn this WILD

Post found
numbers
#LookForNumbers

Create a foot
monster

Add another cat
to the Internet

#POST
THIS
BOOK

Point and snap

BESTIES

#POST THIS BOOK

Express any of these:

TOPPLE! SPIN! JUMP!

#POST THIS BOOK

Capture imagination in this jar

#POST THIS BOOK

 #POST THIS BOOK Open the jar

Point your camera
upward.
Find art in the sky.

POINT 📷
AND SNAP

Point your camera
downward.
Find art on the ground.

Decorate and share
on a Monday #PostThisBook

Show the adventures of a toy

Rearrange flowers

Bling

AND OFF THE PAGE

 Overlap shapes

 USE A NEW
APP OR EFFECT
e.g. levitation, panorama,
pop art, slo-mo,
superimpose

#POST
THIS
BOOK

Create using
bits and bobs

Depict a song without using words

#POST THIS BOOK

GUESS MY SONG

#POST
THIS
BOOK

Whirl your colors

HANDMADE

POINT AND SNAP

Retail therapy

Add real
fabric to
this bag

#POST
THIS
BOOK

#POST
THIS
BOOK

Show something out of place

Turn anything into a unicorn

#SeeTheUnicorns

FROM A BUG'S POINT OF VIEW

#POST THIS BOOK

Film

a journey in

time-lapse

Celebrate a celebrity

#POST
THIS
BOOK

POST THIS TO REACH THE CELEBRITY

An image inspired by #POST THIS BOOK
googling the word PATTERN

CREATE A PATCHWORK
#TheMassiveBlanket

Expand
and
color

Create FAN ART #POST THIS BOOK

NAIL ART

#POST THIS BOOK

↑
Your hand here

Be misguided
with makeup

FILM a THUMB WAR
in costume

A thing in multiple

#POST
THIS
BOOK

ADD AN ABSTRACT EXPRESSION

#POST THIS BOOK

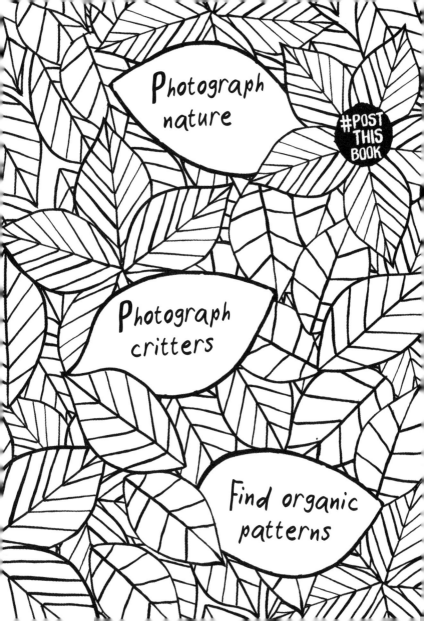

Depict yourself as an animal

FILM IN REVERSE
#PostThisBook

LET LOOSE #POST
HERE THIS
BOOK

#POST
THIS
BOOK

Display your
materials

FAKE A **TATTOO**
YOU'D REGRET

Show lines on
your hand

An Image from My Generation

 Who remembers this?

Color a storm

#POST
THIS
BOOK.

CAKE FACE

POINT
AND SNAP

PANT AND SNAP

POINT AND SNAP

POINT
AND SNAP

DANCING FEET

Share a four-word poem

I award you this for AWESOMENESS

#POST THIS BOOK

Post this to praise someone

Attempt a balancing act

#POST THIS BOOK

Create from any online tutorial

#PostThisBook

Draw on a photograph

#PostThisBook

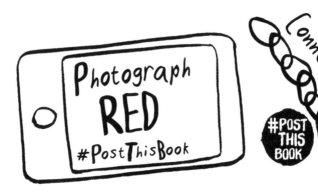

Photograph RED

#PostThisBook

Connect

#POST THIS BOOK

#POST THIS BOOK

Freeze-frame a game

#POST
THIS
BOOK

Make a piece of toast your canvas

BUBBLES

GROTESQUE PORTRAIT

INCOMING!

#POST THIS BOOK

POINT & SNAP

#POST THIS BOOK Fingerprint folk

#POST THIS BOOK HOW MY BRAIN WORKS . . .

YiPPEE it's FRIDAY

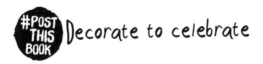

#POST THIS BOOK Decorate to celebrate

 **Expand and color**

RANDOM

#POST THIS BOOK

Point and snap 📷

Blooming colors

Show the breeze

Mummified selfie

REPEAT
REPEAT
REPEAT

Ooze happiness

#POST
THIS
BOOK

What's he looking at?

Take a photo portrait of someone without showing their face

#PostThisBook

STYLE THIS
PAGE

#POST THIS BOOK

Keep something in here #POST THIS BOOK

Film one action. LOOP IT #PostThisBook

Me when I looked different

#POST THIS BOOK

My #PostThisBook workspace

Point and snap

TANGLE THIS PAGE #POST THIS BOOK

EXPAND
and color

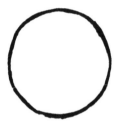

Capture the effects of rain **#POST THIS BOOK**

Utilize a plastic bottle **#POST THIS BOOK**

#POST THIS BOOK

Take your camera for a walk

Add color to a **T**-shirt

Add speech bubbles to an image

MOSAIC FROM FRAGMENTS

#POST
THIS
BOOK

Divide this page

Film water

POUT

📷 POINT

YUMMY!

SHOE SHOT

& SNAP #POST THIS BOOK

LIKE

Do your hair differently

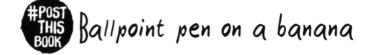

Ballpoint pen on a banana

Add flowers here.
Post this, tagging
a friend who
deserves flowers.

#POST THIS BOOK

Capture
something
beautiful

MY FACE
AS A
CANVAS

Over-decorate
a cupcake

AND OFF THE PAGE

#POST
THIS
BOOK

Find love for your pet at
#PetLoveMatch

PET'S DATING PROFILE

#POST THIS BOOK AMPLIFY this

#POST THIS BOOK

Depict a fictional character from a game, book, or cartoon

LOOK!

IT'S A MEME

Animate an
inanimate object

#PostThisBook

The same but different

↓

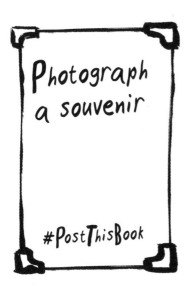

Photograph a souvenir

#PostThisBook

Google the word "art." Share a screenshot.

CREDIT THE SOURCE

#POST THIS BOOK

 Photograph someone taking a photo

Show a Rapid Recipe

#POST
THIS
BOOK

RESPOND ON

Covered in spots

PAPER-BAG
HEAD

BUTTONS

AND OFF **T**HE PAGE

MEMORIES

#PostThisBook

POINT 📷
AND SNAP

TOTES CUTE!

#PostThisBook

USE THIS PAGE TO CONTINUE
ANOTHER PICTURE #POST
THIS
BOOK

THE OOPS! PAGE

#POST THIS BOOK

1. Finish your life's **To Do** list
2.

Remove your shoes

Record a day in snippets #POST THIS BOOK

#POST THIS BOOK Gummy Bear Horror Show

EXPLODE
COLOR #POST
THIS
BOOK

Record laughter

 Present food artistically

FIND A FACE IN AN **O**BJECT

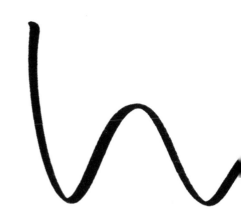

#POST THIS BOOK

Show the death of a tomato

FILM A PART OF YOUR ROUTINE

#POST THIS BOOK

Create
an outfit by
positioning

clothes on
the floor

#PostThisBook

#POST THIS BOOK

Completely
cover an
object in color

Fake an antique photo

RECORD PIECES OF A PLACE

#POST THIS BOOK DISGUISE

POINT AND SNAP

#POST THIS BOOK Origami attempt

#POST THIS BOOK STRIKE A POSE

Odd socks **#POST THIS BOOK**

Point and snap 📷

SHOW A
COLLECTION

Turn a
thing SCARY

Refashion
fashion

#POST
THIS
BOOK

Express any of these: 📽 ✏️✏️

SPLAT! BURST! WOBBLE!

IMITATE SOMEONE ELSE'S WORK THAT YOU LIKE

#POST THIS BOOK

RESPOND ON

Beach art

Yesterday's technology

PRESS
YOUR
FACE

AND OFF **T**HE PAGE

Stick-man tragedy #POST THIS BOOK

Start Here.
Go beyond the
edges of the
book

#POST
THIS
BOOK

#POST THIS BOOK

MESS WITH
THE SCALE
OF **T**HINGS

Use a window
as a frame

Create a ghostly effect

Devise a tabletop obstacle course

 Photograph reflections

 Attempt a tricky throw. Record it.

Photograph a secluded spot

 Time-lapse a TIDY UP

RESPOND ON

A close-up view

Paint a leaf

RECORD A BUILDING

AND OFF THE PAGE

#POST THIS BOOK

AN IMAGE INSPIRED BY
GOOGLING THE WORD

COLOR

#POST
THIS
BOOK

Film
a silent
scream

#POST THIS BOOK

The first item
I'd save from
a fire

📷 Point and snap

Build a badly made model

Capture **SHADOWS**

#POST THIS BOOK

FILM AN ANIMAL

#PostThisBook

Use a boot as a vase

Zombify **#POST THIS BOOK**

something unlikely

#POST
THIS
BOOK

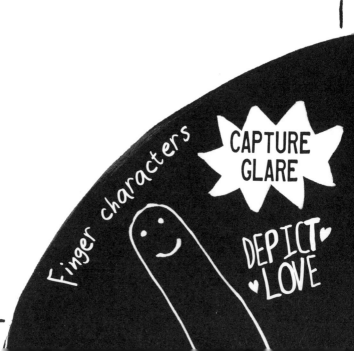

Finger characters

CAPTURE GLARE

DEPICT LOVE

Film a
flick-through
of this book